SUPER SCIENCE FEATS:
MEDICAL BREAKTHROUGHS
X-RAYS

by Alicia Z. Klepeis

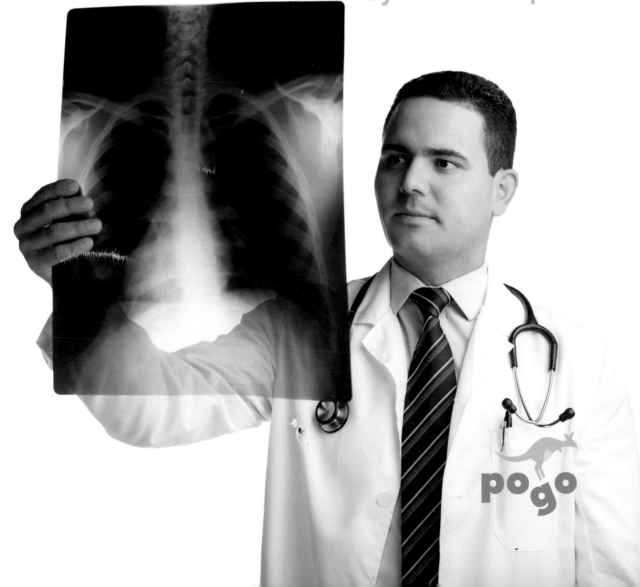

pogo

Ideas for Parents and Teachers

Pogo Books let children practice reading informational text while introducing them to nonfiction features such as headings, labels, sidebars, maps, and diagrams, as well as a table of contents, glossary, and index.

Carefully leveled text with a strong photo match offers early fluent readers the support they need to succeed.

Before Reading

- "Walk" through the book and point out the various nonfiction features. Ask the student what purpose each feature serves.
- Look at the glossary together. Read and discuss the words.

Read the Book

- Have the child read the book independently.
- Invite him or her to list questions that arise from reading.

After Reading

- Discuss the child's questions. Talk about how he or she might find answers to those questions.
- Prompt the child to think more. Ask: What did you know about X-rays before reading this book? What more would you like to learn about them?

Pogo Books are published by Jump!
5357 Penn Avenue South
Minneapolis, MN 55419
www.jumplibrary.com

Library of Congress Cataloging-in-Publication Data

Names: Klepeis, Alicia, 1971– author.
Title: X-rays / by Alicia Z. Klepeis.
Description: Minneapolis, MN: Jump!, Inc., [2021]
Series: Super science feats: medical breakthroughs
Includes index. | Audience: Ages 7-10
Identifiers: LCCN 2020030738 (print)
LCCN 2020030739 (ebook)
ISBN 9781645278047 (hardcover)
ISBN 9781645278054 (paperback)
ISBN 9781645278061 (ebook)
Subjects: LCSH: X-rays–Juvenile literature.
Radiography–Juvenile literature.
Classification: LCC RC78 .K53 2020 (print)
LCC RC78 (ebook) | DDC 616.07/572–dc23
LC record available at https://lccn.loc.gov/2020030738
LC ebook record available at https://lccn.loc.gov/2020030739

Editor: Eliza Leahy
Designer: Michelle Sonnek

Photo Credits: Tridsanu Thopet/Shutterstock, cover; aldomurillo/iStock, 1; Daboost/Shutterstock, 3; Emin Ozkan/Shutterstock, 4; Dragon Images/Shutterstock, 5; Chronicle/Alamy, 6-7; World History Archive/Alamy, 8-9; CPM Photo/Shutterstock, 10 (left); Africa Studio/Shutterstock, 10 (right); Tyler Olson/Shutterstock, 11; Xray Computer/Shutterstock, 12-13; Creativaimages/iStock, 14; Radiography Art/Shutterstock, 15; Charday Penn/iStock, 16-17; Juice Flair/Shutterstock, 18-19; Elnur/Shutterstock, 20-21; itsmejust/Shutterstock, 23.

Printed in the United States of America at Corporate Graphics in North Mankato, Minnesota.

TABLE OF CONTENTS

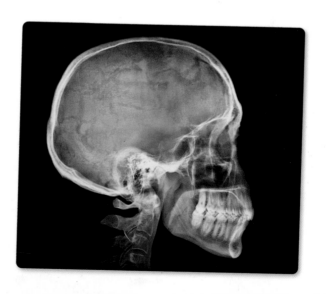

CHAPTER 1

AN INSIDE LOOK

Have you ever had an **X-ray** done? An X-ray is a picture. It shows the inside of your body. Doctors use X-rays to find broken bones.

X-ray

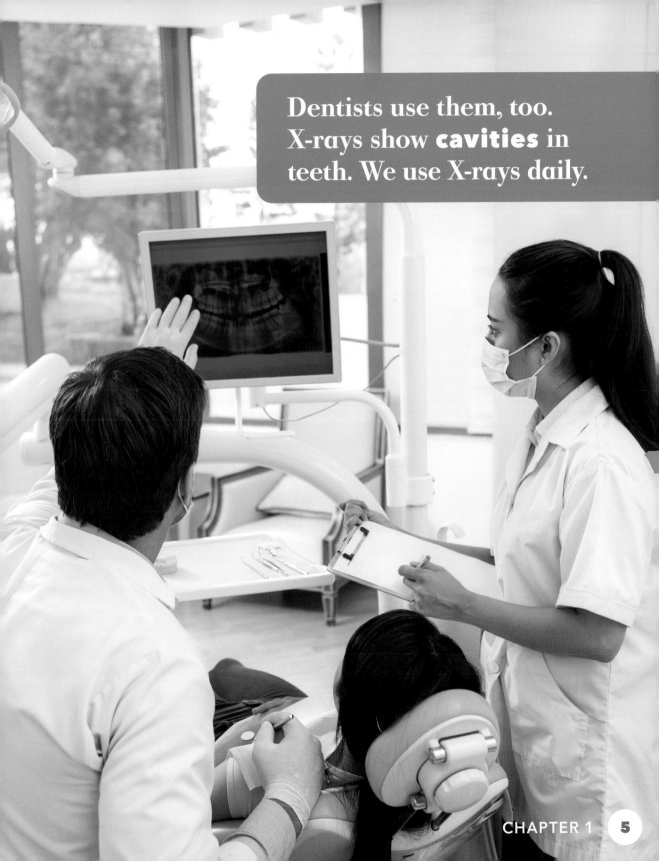

Dentists use them, too. X-rays show **cavities** in teeth. We use X-rays daily.

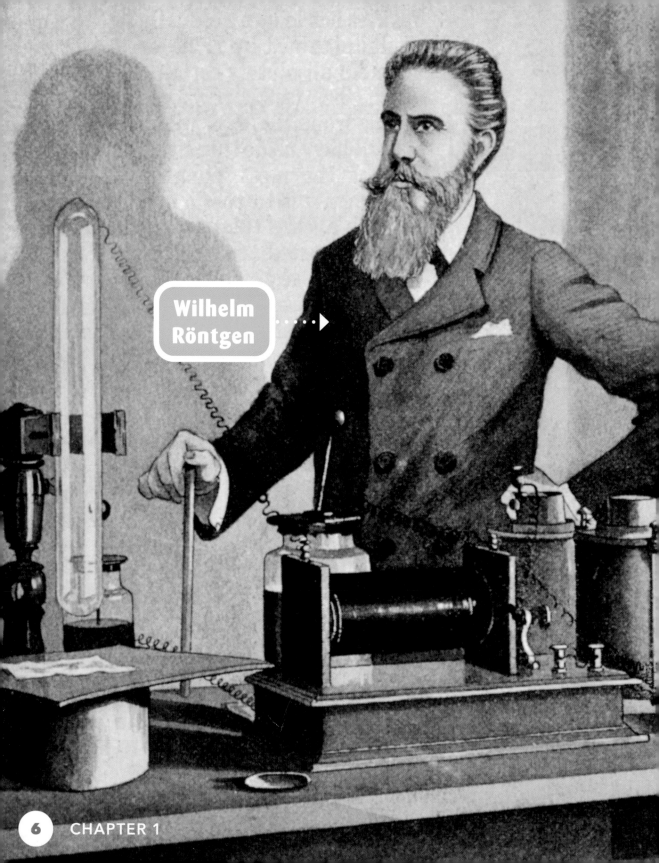

X-rays were discovered by accident in 1895. Wilhelm Röntgen was a scientist. He was studying whether **cathode rays** could pass through glass. These rays are streams of **electrons**. He covered a glass tube in thick black paper. He thought it would keep the rays from escaping. He was wrong.

A nearby **fluorescent** screen lit up. Röntgen figured some invisible rays had escaped from the tube. They caused the glow. He called them "X" rays.

Röntgen kept studying X-rays. They were a type of **radiation**. He found that they could not go through dense objects. But they could go through human **tissue**. This made it possible to see the bones underneath.

News traveled fast. Doctors started using X-rays to help find broken bones and swallowed objects. Before X-rays, doctors had to do **surgery** to find these things. This was a medical **breakthrough**!

DID YOU KNOW?

Pets often swallow objects that are not food. Like what? Toys, socks, and coins are some. Veterinarians use X-rays to find them.

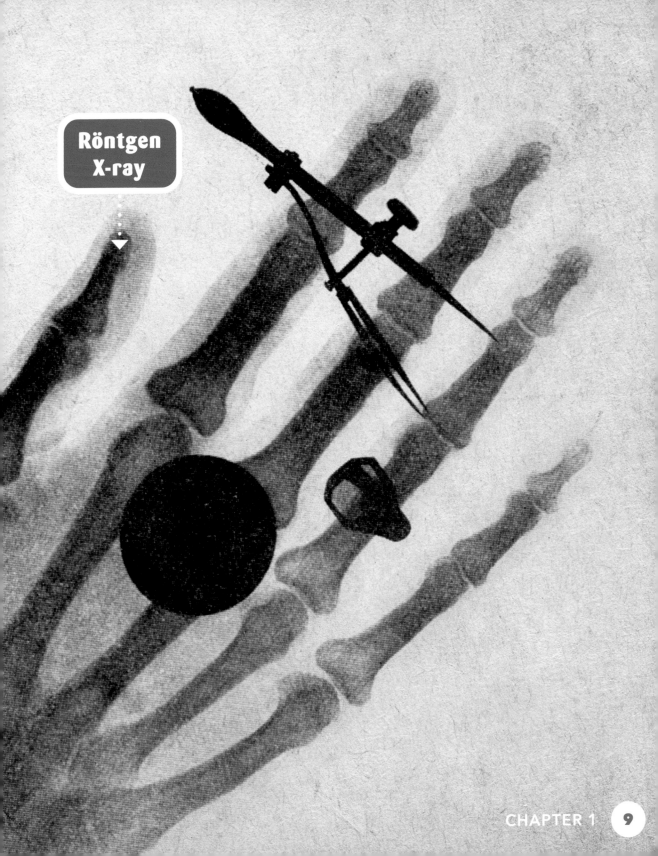

Röntgen
X-ray

CHAPTER 2

HOW X-RAYS WORK

X-rays are a form of radiation, just like visible light. But they can pass through your skin. Have you ever made shadow pictures on a wall? Your hand stops some light rays. But some pass through your skin. You might see it glow.

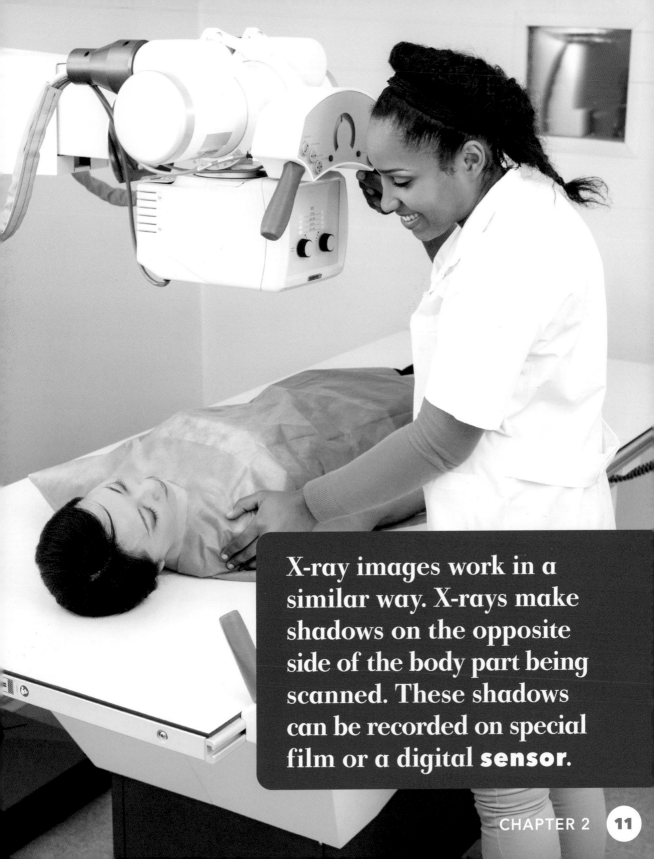

X-ray images work in a similar way. X-rays make shadows on the opposite side of the body part being scanned. These shadows can be recorded on special film or a digital **sensor**.

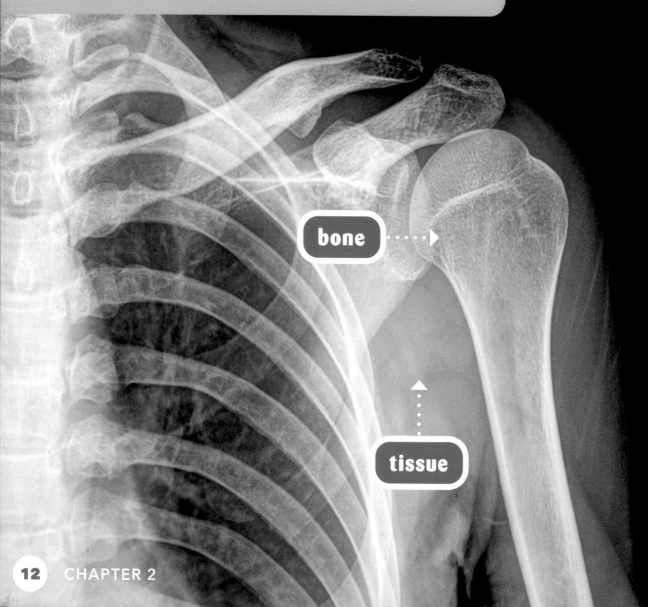

Fat and skin do not block much of an X-ray beam. Muscle blocks more. Bones block X-rays well. Why? They are dense. This makes them show up clearly on X-ray images.

bone ·····▶

tissue

TAKE A LOOK!

How do X-ray machines work? Take a look!

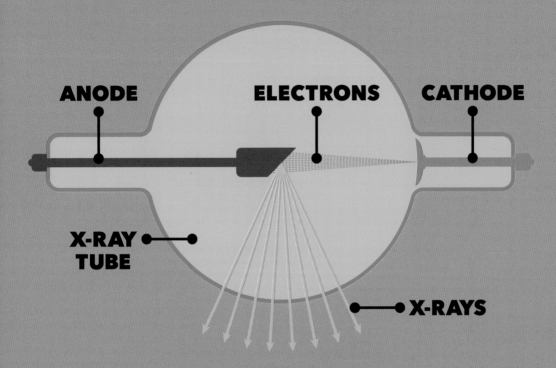

ANODE **ELECTRONS** **CATHODE**

X-RAY TUBE

X-RAYS

① The machine contains an X-ray tube. Electrons hit the **anode**. This makes X-rays.

② The **cathode** focuses the X-rays in a beam. It aims the beam at the anode.

③ The X-rays focus on a part of the body. An image is made.

CHAPTER 3

X-RAYS TODAY

Let's say you hurt your leg while riding your bike. You're afraid it might be broken.

You go to the hospital for an X-ray. You put on a heavy apron. Why? It protects you from radiation. Too much can be bad for you.

X-ray images show the doctor if a bone is broken. But X-rays can find other things, too. They can help find **diseases** such as cancer and COVID-19.

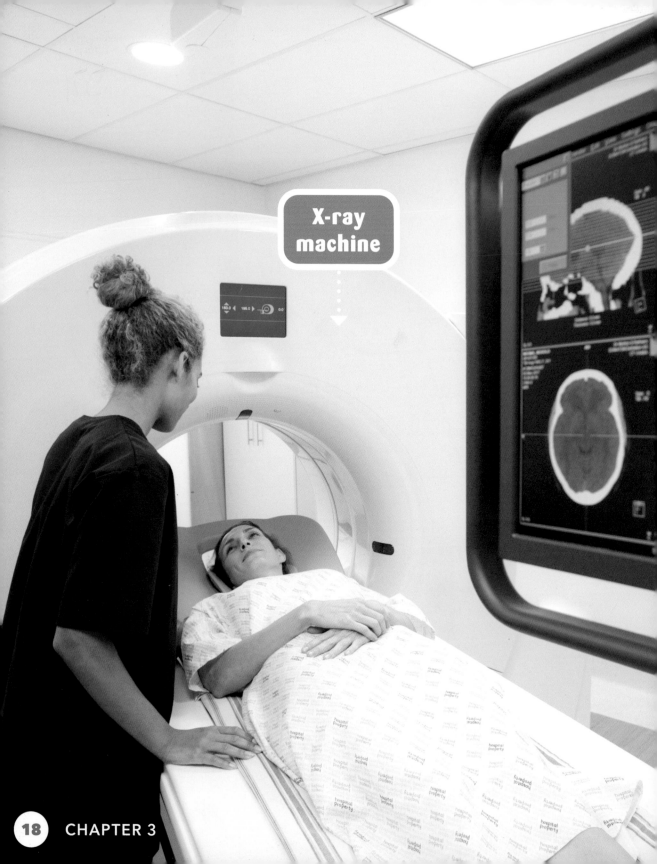

X-ray
machine

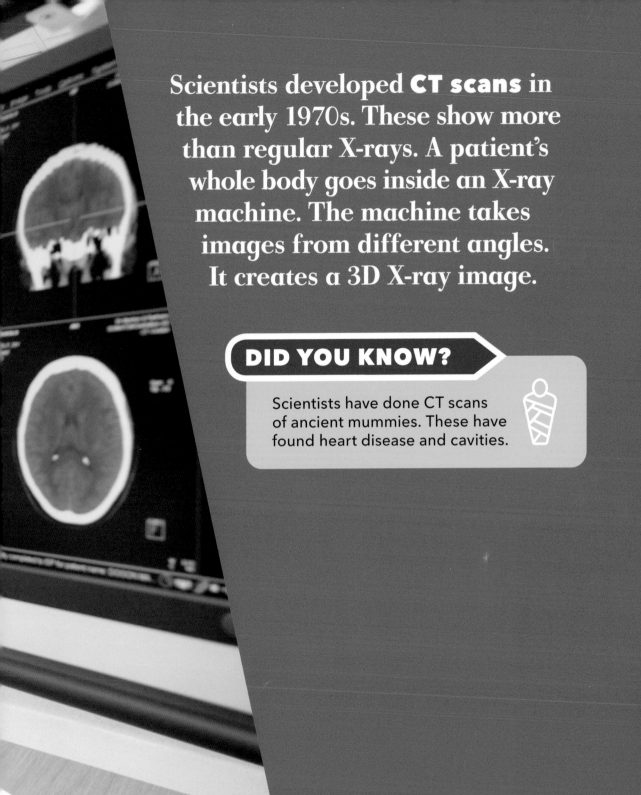

Scientists developed **CT scans** in the early 1970s. These show more than regular X-rays. A patient's whole body goes inside an X-ray machine. The machine takes images from different angles. It creates a 3D X-ray image.

DID YOU KNOW?

Scientists have done CT scans of ancient mummies. These have found heart disease and cavities.

X-rays give us a look inside our bodies. They help find injuries and diseases. They keep us healthy. They save lives.

ACTIVITIES & TOOLS

MAKE A MOCK X-RAY

X-rays help us see inside the human body. Find out more about the bones in your hand with this activity.

What You Need:
- white chalk
- black construction paper
- computer or tablet
- scissors
- Q-tips
- glue

❶ Using the chalk, trace the outline of your hand on the paper. Keep your fingers spread apart.

❷ Research what bones are in your hand. There are 27 in all!

❸ Cut the Q-tips to create each of the "bones."

❹ Glue the bones in their correct locations.

GLOSSARY

anode: The part inside an X-ray tube that attracts electrons.

breakthrough: An important discovery or advance in knowledge.

cathode: The part inside an X-ray tube that sends out electrons.

cathode rays: Streams of electrons seen in vacuum tubes; they carry electric current through the tube.

cavities: Holes in teeth that have been hollowed out by decay.

CT scans: X-ray images made when a computer combines multiple X-ray images to show a part of an object or a person's body.

diseases: Sicknesses, especially ones with specific symptoms or which affect a specific part of the body.

electrons: Tiny particles of atoms that have negative charges of electricity.

fluorescent: Producing visible light when exposed to external radiation.

radiation: The process of giving off energy in the form of particles or waves.

sensor: A device that detects a physical property and records it.

surgery: Medical treatment that involves repairing, removing, or replacing injured or diseased parts of the body, usually by cutting.

tissue: A layer or mass of cells that forms the basic structural materials of a person's body.

X-ray: A type of radiation that can pass through many materials, or the image formed by using this type of energy.

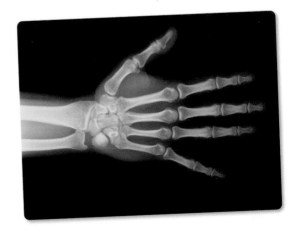

INDEX

TO LEARN MORE

Finding more information is as easy as 1, 2, 3.

1 Go to www.factsurfer.com

2 Enter "X-rays" into the search box.

3 Choose your book to see a list of websites.

FACT SURFER

MB

DEC - - 2021